A Collection

Poems

by

Joan Fitzgerald

Buffalo Arts Publishing

A Collection, Poems by Joan Fitzgerald. Copyright © 2018 by Joan Fitzgerald. All rights reserved. Printed in the United States of America. No part of this book may be used or reproduced in any manner whatsoever without written permission from the publisher. For information, address Buffalo Arts Publishing, 179 Greenfield Drive, Tonawanda, NY 14150.

Email: info@buffaloartspublishing.com

ISBN 978-0997874174 | LCCN 2018902530

Front cover image: *Gemini II*, 2010, by Joan Fitzgerald
Back cover image: *Defiance*, 2012, by Joan Fitzgerald

Printed in the USA

Acknowledgements

Livestock, **ARTVOICE**, Buffalo, New York
The End of August, **ARTVOICE**, Buffalo, New York
The Pacifist (as *Peace on Earth*), **ARTVOICE**, Buffalo, New York
Requiem (Anniversary), **Dan River Anthology**, Thomaston, Maine
Procession, **Raven Chronicles**, Seattle, Washington
Night Sounds, **ARTVOICE**, Buffalo, New York
Heaven's Tourists, **The Buffalo News**, Buffalo, New York
The Fireman, **ARTVOICE**, Buffalo, New York
            The SOW'S EAR, Donalds, South Carolina
Talisman, **ARTVOICE**, Buffalo, New York
Breakwall, **The Buffalo News**, Buffalo, New York
Happy Marriage, **Northwoods Journal**, Thomaston, Maine
Tarnished Glass, **Northwoods Journal**, Thomaston, Maine
            (winner of the 2005 poetry contest)
The Country People, **Northwoods Journal**, Thomaston, Maine

Contents

Love Letters

    Sisters 9
    Reading Emily Dickinson 9
    Five Houses 10
    Rayette 10
    The Invitation 11
    Invisible 11
    Invention 12
    Siren 12
    Sixteen Years Later 13
    Costumes 14
    Hot 14

Others

    Four o'clock 17
    Nice Things 20
    Testosterone 23
    Adult Education 25
    Karma 28
    Beauty 29
    Waiting 31
    A Drowning 33
    Looking Backward 34
    Persephone 37
    The Journey 38
    Waiting for Santa 40

Family Snapshots 41
The Watchers 43
The Illusionist 45
A Refusal to Mutate 49

Glamour

Livestock 53
The End of August 55
The Pacifist 57
Blood Line 58
Tiffany and Beauty 60
Anniversary 62
Glamour 64
The Little Toad 66
Procession 68
Procession II 70
Round and Round 72
Night Sounds 75
Heaven's Tourists 76
The Fireman 78
Waiting for Spring 79
Talisman 82
Starstruck 83
Summer Kisses 85
Saturday Morning 88

The Sweet Life

- Breakwall 93
- Happy Marriage 95
- Noel, Noel 97
- Tarnished Glass 100
  - ——*Gene* 100
  - ——*Bobby* 103
  - ——*Frank* 106
- Black Horses 109
- The Country People 112
- The Sweet Life 114
- Rural Distinction 116
- Charade 118
- Passages 122
- Meat 125
- Tunnel Vision 128
- Just Before the House Blew Up 131

Love Letters

Sisters

You should not have all those sisters,
fattish, popcorn-smeared girls,
crackling flesh stuffed into tiny bikinis
prancing around a bonfire,
ignoring your sea-raked eyes,
the moonlight blackness of your hair.
Forget them!
I will be your sister.
We will dance slowly on the embracing sand.

Reading Emily Dickinson

"Sex is more fun than poetry," she observed
to her lover of the month,
flinging down the book.
"A loaded gun indeed!"
Later,
in post-tumescent wonder,
he commented:
"You're so experienced."
"No,
I simply read a lot of poetry."

Five Houses

Was it her black-circled eyes, the cigarette cough
or her addled housekeeping
that enticed him to leave four children and a wife?
And did she groan with pleasure at his rotund form
posing on a dirt bike
as she abandoned two teen-agers and a spouse.
 "We've got five houses now," she announced years later,
but would that ever be enough?

Rayette

When her hormones settled down,
she stopped getting drunk in the lake shore bars,
drag racing on country roads or
clutching some man's back on a motorcycle
and got a job in a drug store,
where she was known as dependable and helpful.
She never regretted one wild minute,
but sometimes,
she rued the tattoos.

The Invitation

"An artist, you say?"
He looked furtively about.
"Tell me —
Have you ever drawn a naked man?"
"Many times —
art school, life classes, workshops."
His smile became a leer.
"Want to go out for a drink?"

Invisible

She is hiding,
far down in the layers of somnolence
like a guttering candle.
If she doesn't move,
no one will see her

Outside the room,
hawks and owls crash
in the carnivorous night.

Invention

After losing her upper teeth
and not having dental insurance,
Pauline fashioned a replica out of canning wax,
anchored it to her gums with Denture-Grip.
Now, her husband feels no embarrassment
when they go to the tavern on Saturday night.

Siren

Why did she imagine that giving herself freely
on every first date
would stun a man into the long walk to the altar?
Scared off by her sexual prowess,
they left immediately
or stayed around long enough to borrow money.
Tiffany was never to be surprised by an engagement ring.

Sixteen Years Later

A pink chiffon gown, white gardenias,
her date's black tuxedo
fluttered in her head like
a cloud of gorgeous moths.
The Junior Prom.

"Oh please, mother, say that I can go.
I have to be there!
Some of us will rent a limo and
we'll go out for breakfast in the morning.
Please! Please!"

"Don't be stupid!
I went to my Junior Prom and I got you!
You are not going!"

Costumes

He loved wearing her special black bikini underwear around the house
and at Halloween parties
he was Madonna, Lady Ga Ga
and once, Gypsy Rose Lee.
Magenta lipstick staining his mustache,
size-thirteen feet with purple toenails forced into strappy sandals,
chest hair peeking through beige lace.
His wife thought that there were worse things.

Hot

Her fluorescent, incandescent, effervescent past
boiled in the sauce pot.
The swollen lid spilling brown steam,
green froth the color of turtles,
glittering purple bubbles,
and the odor of cheap aftershave and sweat.
She kept it in the cellar of her mind.

Others

Four o'clock

Black snow
in the glittering, reflected light of December.
A late afternoon.

Jason's truck rocketed over the packed ice.
He had come from Sullivan's Tavern,
stopped after work
to see the pretty, blond barmaid,
talk to her a little,
have a few beers.
Things were going along smoothly until
some guys he knew started in on him.
"Hey Potholes," they called.
"Trying to get a date?"
The barmaid went to serve people at the other end of the bar
and that was that.

It was because of his skin.
Acne-scarred, purple with eruptions.
He thought that maybe she wouldn't mind,
but with that nickname —

It was terribly cold.
Frost covered the windshield.

To his right, there were skid marks and a car off in the field
crumpled at a funny angle,
its hood bisected by a tree.

He pulled over, got out, curious,
walked through the snow to get a better look.
Inside the car, a man was crushed against the steering wheel,
no air bag,
his head a terrible mess.

Jason looked around swiftly.
There was little traffic on this desolate road.
Birds shrieked over his shoulder
as he slid his hand into the car, shrinking from the carnage,
exploring pockets.
The back one yielded a wallet.
He drew it out and opened it —
A few bills, credit cards — forget that.
Then a pay check.
The check was beige, rectangular, listing deductions, overtime, taxes,
more money than he made in a month as a laborer for the village.
Hurrying, he stuffed it in his jacket,
dropped the wallet in the frozen mud near the door of the vehicle,
scuffed snow over his footprints leading to the car.

Darkness was falling like a blanket of ink when he took off.
The pick-up truck going too fast, shimmying.
Got to calm down,
these roads were bad, rutted.
He'd drive down to Cranston,

no one knew him there, cash the check at the Citizen's Bank,
find a doctor to fix his face.
Sanding — that's what they did now,
or some kind of red light therapy.
Everything would be all right.

But somehow,
he knew that it wouldn't be.

Nice Things

So easy for Brenda to enthrall the shy forty-year-old bachelor,
smiling, as she presented
her luminescent breasts.
Bert was smitten.
She was his first real girlfriend.
That she was a widow with three children,
lived unhappily with her parents, worked part-time,
didn't matter.
She opened the door to experiences that he had only imagined.

On her husband's last splintered Friday,
black ice, frantic steering,
the car lying dismembered against a tree,
Brenda had paced nervously, screaming at the kids,
checked phone messages,
descended into hysteria.
"Instantaneous," the policeman said,
returning his things to her.
There was blood on the wallet, the medical cards, but no pay check.
"Who would steal a paycheck off a dead man?
That was the rent check," she sobbed,
before moving in with her parents.

She taught Bert how to drink cocktails,
to manage a self-conscious sort of dancing
in the soiled glamor of the local bars,

full of heavy drinkers, snow mobile enthusiasts,
women who counted on being drunk
every night by one o'clock.
She was known in these places.

Her father issued a curfew when she came home
smeared, tipsy, unfocused,
the sun painting the rooftops with gold.
"My house! My rules!"

The children made her mother nervous.
"Lola Sue sassed me again.
You have to speak to her.
I'm running out of patience."

She dreamed of her own home, saw herself entering the door,
arms full of daffodils,
beaming at the matching maroon couch and chairs,
patterned rugs, tufted pillows,
arranging her everyday dishes.
"Bert is serious," she confided to her best friend, Mary Louise.
"But he wants to wait until we've saved enough money to have nice things
before there's an engagement."

The wait was driving Brenda crazy.
Her parents were becoming more critical, exacting.
"I'm pregnant!" she confided to Mary Louise.
"What does Bert think?"

"I haven't told him yet."
"You'd better do it soon before someone else does."
She wore a blue, lace-trimmed dress, cut very low,
plied him with Southern Comfort Old Fashioned cocktails,
and whispered the news.
He stared at her in disbelief.
"I don't believe it! You assured me —"
"Nothing's one hundred percent," she protested.
"You're calling me a bastard maker!" he exploded.
"But honey," she implored.
"We are through!" He stormed out.

A month later, she told her friend:
"I lost it! I went down to the cellar,
heaved up a big dresser and walked it around the furnace all evening
until I could barely stand.
My stomach hurt so bad that I wanted to die.
The next day the bleeding started."

Mary Louise knew that there had been no pregnancy.

Brenda did not see her boyfriend again.
She took to staring numbly at nothing.
Instead of daffodils, she saw the years smeared on the walls
with dirty charcoal,
the weeks dropping to the floor like bricks.

Bert married a woman that he met at the library.
They live in Cincinnati.

Testosterone

Darleen was enchanted by his perfect profile,
the beautifully delineated nose, marble-like chin, glossy brow,
which he presented for her worshipful gaze,
elevating his head slightly from his bronzed neck,
powerful shoulders,
and letting the sun illuminate it.

They lived together.

Slowly, she became aware that despite the profile,
Carl had a tendency for violent acts.
At her cousin's wedding reception, he hurled the groom's father
into a musical trio playing Hava Negila
because the man told Carl:
"You do the twist like a constipated monkey!"

A week later, he head-butted his uncle and stomped on him
while they were working on a motorcycle in the garage
for calling him a shitty loser when he quit his job abruptly.

Darleen thought a lot about these incidents
as she progressed in her Dental Hygiene program at the community
college, which he had paid for,
while delicately probing for cavities with her silver pick,
but she still had one semester left.

He choked and socked his best friend during a bar fight

after a lot of beer when the friend had hot words
about Carl's favorite football team,
the one whose Quarterback's jersey he wore four days a week.

The end arrived after her graduation ceremony
where he argued ominously with her college advisor,
fists flexed, chest heaving,
because Darleen had been forced to take remedial algebra.

When the advisor decked him,
he landed face down in a punch bowl
and they left immediately.
The flawless profile was slightly damaged.
The nose slid to one side.
She examined it critically, but it was definitely not the same.

She packed all her possessions,
clothes, stuffed-animals, jewelry, her grandmother's silver bracelet,
tossed everything into the back seat of the car that he had bought for her
and hit the expressway for the next city,
where a job awaited in the Smile Time Dental Clinic.

Finding her gone, Carl punched holes in the drywall,
burned down the shed and broke some windows.
Then, he went out to look for a girl who might be
enthralled by an almost perfect profile
and liked to witness occasional physical drama.

Adult Education

Natalia keeps her eyes on the instructor
never looks down toward the bulges, the jiggling bosoms
of her own torso encased in black tights and a magenta tee shirt,
as she tap dances
in a line of overweight, over-bleached ladies
with exploded veins stumbling around the floor.
She watches Miss Tina,
endlessly preppy, slim, in purple leotards as she barks out commands.

KICK-BALL CHANGE! STEP AND TURN!
KICK-BALL CHANGE! STEP AND TURN!

Natalia always had headaches,
wore her waist-length, glossy hair
in a large coil.
Headaches every day until her doctor
suggested having it cut shorter,
perhaps her head wouldn't hurt so much.
She hated it short.
It wasn't her.
A small head with Madonna features over a pillowy body,
bisected by her corset.
She bought a false bun and pinned it on,
looked somewhat as she used to.
The headaches persisted.

TAP! TAP! TAP!
TAP! TAP! TAP!

Her husband did not make her happy.
He invested in horses, dog races, prize fights, poker games,
a portly, little man in a cream-colored sports jacket,
slipping out the door in his panama hat,
heading for the track, any track as she screamed at him:
"You don't live right!"

and besides, there were no thrills.
She thought his penis was too small.
Her headaches increased.

TAP! TAP! TAP!
TAP! TAP! TAP!

She once had a beauticians license,
worked for an undertaker
doing hair and make-up on the departed
but made an early mistake
when she mixed up the guests and
gave a curly perm and a full, dramatic make-up to a man.
She wasn't fired until the funeral director
caught her raising the sheet to check out a client's private parts.
She was right about her husband.

TAP! TAP! TAP!

Her sons married girls that she hated.
They refused to name their daughters after her or her mother.
It was traditional, for God's sake!
What kind of names were Shauna and Brenna?

Not in her family!
And they called her Gran,
not Grandmama or even Nana.
Skinny, little sticks! They made her nervous,
lived on chips and hot pockets.

ROCKETTES!
ROCKETTES!

She clamps her arms on the shoulders on the women on either side
and kicks in time with the clumsy, out-of-step dancers.
Her kicks are always the highest.
Twice a week, she comes to class,
full of determination, seething with energy.
The headaches are gone.

Karma

Beyond the time
of keeping horses in the barn
living on the crust of the hill
standing neck-deep in a cold creek
among sun-shards on the water
leaping from river-washed stone to stone

mad April

Shacks shanties A frames
rotted farm houses that exploded
yards full of broken refrigerators sofas garbage
dogs howling in pulsating nights
dead rabbits
falling into unexpected holes
guns and bullets
while the deer ran and ran

hex signs stiff against the trees
drinking up the moon in country taverns
wanting
wanting
beyond any way back
no entry through
bridges rock-strewn paths
under extinguished stars
the sun is black

Beauty

The newlyweds: so dazzling in the wedding
announcement page of the Sunday paper.
She wore an ivory lace, strapless gown accented with crystal beads
complementing her glossy, black hair.
The groom was outfitted in the family kilt
displaying his muscular legs.
Smiling, exhibiting perfect teeth,
they trivialized the other marriage announcements.

And when their friends visited the couple's new home,
they expected a triumph of taste,
comfortable, welcoming, unique,
so like the beautiful pair.

It was bewilderingly ugly.
Only a numbness to décor
could produce garish industrial-strength shag carpeting,
sleazy chintz slipcovers,
Lucite chairs, gold-leaf mirrors,
white plaster poodles crouched on a lipstick-pink mantle,
numbing chartreuse wallpaper printed with images
insect-devouring plants.
The guests gasped as they were served box wine
and cheese whiz on saltines.

Surely, the children would be exquisite reproduction
of their photogenic parents.

graceful, elfin, charming as only fortunate offspring could be.
They were beyond homely.
Awkward, gap-toothed, knobby-kneed, lazy-eyed, sparse-haired,
their legs so uneven that they walked on a slant.
Relatives wondered if the wrong babies
had been given out at the hospital.

At school conference night,
the teachers waited nervously for the parents of these gnomes to arrive.

Would they be chewing tobacco? Clad in a stained house dress and cuffed
overalls? Boots fragrant with manure? Obscenely fat? Drunk?

The beautiful couple swept in, impossible as royalty,
illuminating the mundane classroom with their magnetism.
Bringing with them showers of stars, the scent of peonies,
the clearness of bottomless lakes —
to ask:
"Tell us about our adorable, adorable children!"

Waiting

A time of hawks
and the springtime blue of the lake
painted with a rough brush.
No remembrance of the recent shore awash with driftwood,
an upwelling of bones,
old window frames, broken dishes, parts of trees,
sharp-edged seashells
that shattered on the rocks.
The smell of crab apples along the road sweet enough to drive you mad.

And before that —
frozen piles of ice,
absolute and rigid,
voices ringing in the membranous air
as people tried to walk out on the rotted ice
and sank,
knees to waist to shoulders
under black, foreboding clouds.

Or of the autumn.
Ghost ships heading for a vanished amusement park,
a tinkle of pianos beyond the jetty,
laughter,
before the winds began to gather.

Now,
light trembles on boats in the sun-shot harbor.
Wet sand is etched with the pattern of bird's feet, a forgotten scarf.
The beach lies powdery and wanton,
drenched with amnesia
under a remote, pink sky.

A Drowning

The body flung onto the sour boards of the pier,
A bruised flower,
its neck cyanotic
face blue as acid —
pale buttocks caught in a net of seaweed,
surrounded by motionless firemen,
the rescue squad,
an ambulance with open doors.

High on the cliffs
above the mud-colored river
near a frozen custard stand
and the Sea Breeze Amusement Park,
birds slice through the reverberating music
of the Merry-Go-Round,
cars accelerate, race toward the splintered light.

Looking Backward

The villagers always understood.
They knew that the Indian farmhands should be isolated
in their filthy shack of a bar
near the creek,
and that the only blacks in town were cleaning women,
that many years ago,
when the locally elected judge
burned a cross in his front yard
because he hated the Polish,
it was understood.
But when Floyd Baumen rented his late mother's farmhouse
on the main road
across from the Rainbow's End Tavern
to two lesbians from the city,
it was not understood.
The villagers stopped buying him drinks,
did not patronize his septic-tank cleaning service
(Bauman's Honey Dippers)
and kicked him off the bowling team.
Volunteer Firemen attempted to peer into the girl's rooms
from the firehouse next door.
The Lesbians glued glued newspaper over all the windows of the house
and admitted no one.
They loved nature and went for long walks in the woods,
identified birds, took pictures.
Phallic vegetables were deposited at their back door:

cucumbers, crook-necked squashes, oversized carrots.
The girls threw them on the compost pile.
A teen-age clerk at the Stop N' Shop was cool to them,
but curious.
One murky night,
the saloon bulging,
the road thumping with hot noise,
beer fumes pouring out the front door
near a parking lot jammed with pickup trucks,
Maureen Polansky left the bar
after an argument with her husband,
walked unsteadily down the side of the road.
A speeding car,
the driver out of his mind on something,
struck her and flipped her onto the gravel where she lay still,
before he clipped a phone pole and raced off.
The girls heard the crash and ran out of the farmhouse.
One carried a blanket to cover Maureen and ward off shock,
The other called the State Police on her cell phone.
They stayed with her,
kneeling on the tarry surface.
Maureen's husband, Clarence, came looking for his wife
and spotted the group.
He crouched with them and sobbed
until the police and the ambulance came,
the night red with lights and sirens.
After that,
the villagers left tomatoes, pumpkins, fresh eggs at the back door,

ready to embrace them into the Ladies Auxiliary,
the Baseball Appreciation Club.
The Lesbians threw the produce onto the compost,
ripped the newspapers off the windows,
packed their things
and drove back to the city.

Persephone

She is still cocooned,
not ready to make the air fragrant
and exchange gray juncos for brilliant orioles.

Far in the deep hills
surrounded by the thunderous beauty
of trees, rocks, creeks,
a house sits near ditches full of mud
wreathed in the inhaled fierceness of manure,
its porch covered with
broken refrigerators and rusted Christmas tree lights.

She stays unnoticed in a root cellar
beneath rotted floor boards
while up in the living room
obese men in stained overalls clutch cans of beer
and stare at a huge television set that covers the wall.
A woman fries sausages in the kitchen.

Gently rocking, she hums
as boys shoot deer from a pickup truck,
and dogs savage a rabbit.

She waits,
thinking of distant stars, while outside in the gelid weeds
a white horse runs in circles
near the thin crust of April.

The Journey

Cocky as astronauts, they tramped into the Pine Top Bar,
snowmobile suits unzipped, heavy boots dripping.
Their flushed faces full of sweat and cold air,
for a moment diverting attention from the fiddle player on the platform,
the country western dancers kicking and stomping,
diners eating beef and weck, fried shrimp.
Ranging around the bar, they gulped down cold, frothy beer,
sausages from jars, nuts,
drank another round, talking excitedly,
then filing out the door to rev up the motors, lights flashing,
streaking across the highway through the woods onto the trail
panicking the restless deer,
startling the somnambulate birds,
roaring through the darkened night
past stands of evergreens rigid in the reflected snow.

Miles down another trail to a roadhouse on the highway,
its parking lot full of motorcycles.
Inside, tattooed bikers draped in crosses and chains,
eyed them suspiciously
as they nervously stalked into the back room.
The waitress, her false eyelashes wet with mascara, missing some teeth,
took their order, brought foaming pitchers
while they ignored the hoots, the remarks from the bar,
left damp money in a pool of beer.

Next stop was an ancient tavern, a dusty place.
Their machines were left in the deserted parking lot
like a cluster of beetles before they tracked crunchy snow inside
where a few old men nodded.
Snarling animal heads were carved into the mantle behind the bar.
They settled on the warm stools like plump chickens
in this quiet place full of disinfectant smells and age,
draft beer all around,
then back out to the vehicles.

This time running parallel to the road
cutting across pastures and a frozen creek near black barns,
broken wheat stalks in the shuddering night.
Past long deserted-farms, fire-gutted buildings, a brackish pond,
miles of nothing,
climbing higher to the top of the hill,
then plunging down, precipitously, into a valley aching with moonlight,
lost summer cabins, a brutal rock-filled stream,
beyond a bridge painted blue.

Arriving at a small country tavern
where snow-frosted picnic tables lay overturned in the congealed mud.
Apprehensively, they walked to the door, pulled the handle,
but it was locked.
Freezing in the deserted lot, they noticed the absence of cars,
the strangeness of the light, the awful quiet.
Hastily, they got back on the snowmobiles
for the return trip.

Waiting for Santa

His fat black boots
kick at the horned beasts
as he sits
with his foul beard
above the sky
hurling boxes full of
styrofoam, plastic and endangered wood
at the blocked chimneys
causing conflagrations,
infanticides, vendettas, incestuous stabbings,
while we stand
in the cold, cold, gelid air
looking for a sled in the sky.

Family Snapshots

Dolly,
Irish, fertile, red-haired,
produced nine children before her first husband,
Mr. Nolan, passed away.
Soon after,
captivated by her fecundity and her blue eyes,
Mr. Pinckey married her.
They had nine more.
Farm people —
working among the cows, horses, chickens
in the fly-addled barns,
chopping the baked soil of the gardens.
A tough life.
To lighten the drudgery of their endless days,
the older girls played a game with the latest baby
in the kitchen full of wood smoke, canning jars, wash tubs,
tossing him gleefully
from one to the other, dropping him.
The other boys grew up,
won scholarships, became dentists, sportswriters, accountants.
They were intelligent.
None decided on farming.
The girls married, not too badly,
except for Margaret Nolan
who was enticed by Adelarde, an alcoholic, illegal alien,
a French chef full of charm and cooking sherry.

Margaret's sister-in-law took care of the irascible, twice-widowed Dolly
after her diabetic legs were amputated at the thigh.
Demanding, cranky,
she spent her days in a wheel chair
glaring out the window.
Her life was long.
At her funeral,
The priest consoled Evelyn.
"Don't feel sad, my dear. You'll see her in heaven."
"Oh, God!" Evelyn cried. "I hope not!

The Watchers

Above a small, city park near the fire station,
maples and pines lie bare in the winter dusk
as a vast congregation of birds
waits in the snowy branches,
silent, invisible.

Near buildings far over the street,
rows of women huddle before computer screens,
their backs against the night-distorted windows.

Near the bus terminal,
lights blink inside a Burger King.
Across the square, a metro train
spills passengers into the sagging, amethyst evening.

Agitated,
their eyes glittering in trembling feathers,
the birds sense a signal.
Abruptly, they lift off,
hurl themselves against the aluminum air.

A widening net strains birds from the trees,
gathers them into a fist
that bursts skyward
then plunges down to the littered pavement.

The dazzled flock rises,
soars between buildings,
breaks off,
races to the branches
with uncontrolled excitement.

Again and again the swarm lifts,
unites, splits, whirls
enters the shattered light.

The women in the cubicles turn off coffee pots,
close their desks, lock up,
heading for the parking lots.

The firemen magnetize their ears
hoping for the crackle of flames,
rub at specks on the trucks,
yawn.

The birds spring upward,
pulling the air into turbulent eddies
before plummeting.

The metro train creeps, glowing,
it's incandescent skeleton
moving slowly into the purple night.

The Illusionist

Black roses bloomed in his brain,
their petals slowly expanding
in the darkened room where
Rachmaninoff vibrated.
As the music climaxed, the flowers ripened,
he removed the earphones
turned on the lights,
donned his white coat and strode to the door of the office.

To the patients
who had waited for hours
among tattered *Field and Stream* and smudged *Home and Gardens*,
coughing and spitting, flushed,
while the nurses reported
"An emergency at the hospital. He'll be here soon"
(they would quit later in the evening.)

"The doctor will see you, Mrs. Costello. Mr. Davidovich?
You and your son are in room three."
The morphine-engorged doctor faced a patient whose eyes protruded
unnaturally.
"Yes, Mrs. Costello. Allergies!"
"But I'm losing a pound a day!" she protested.
"I said you have allergies!"
He threw a handful of medicine samples at her.
They drifted through the air

like paper violets
as he stormed from the room.
Mr Davidovich patted his son's arm.
"He has a fever, sore throat, cough."
"Yes. An antibiotic." The needle was poised.
"My son is very sensitive about injections."
"Grow up! This will hurt! Only babies cry!"

The child howled as the needle plunged into his arm.
"Idiot!"

The doctor decided to divorce his wife,
(she could keep their six children)
and marry the neighbor down the street, a champion golfer.
A divorce party would be hosted.
The gala was attended by the new fiancée, his bewildered children,
their school friends, deliciously scandalized neighbors and fifty
acquaintances (the house was large.)
He preened, back slapped.
It was a boisterous evening.

Shrimp, avocados, bits of sushi were smeared on the pegged cherry
floors, glasses crashed, paper streamers ripped.
Hours, later, after a good jolt of morphine,
he noticed the knobby tennis-ball calves of his fiancée,
the pre-cancerous lesions on her weathered shoulders,
sun-baked hair clattering like straw as she blew him a celebratory kiss.

It took all his charm to persuade his wife to agree to the reconciliation.

The state revoked his medical certification.
"Local drug-addicted doctor loses license," the paper screamed.
He became interested in horses.
There were plenty of outbuildings on the property.
(thank god for family money — hers.)
Blond horses, black, piebald, short horses for the smaller children.
A retired race horse called to him
across the wet grass every dappled morning.
After a wonderful hit,
he brought them oats.

The family rode in the afternoon with their instructor.
He held his wife's hand as he bounced in the saddle next to her mount.
His tetanus shot had not been updated since childhood.
It was not the sort of injection he was interested in.
He was arrogant, mucking out the barn, stumbling over riding boots.

There was nothing to be done when he fell ill.
Lockjaw was not a pretty way to go.

Within the church organ's blare — loud enough to be Catholic,
the reverend faced the congregation.
He was able to dodder on about subsidized medicine, charter schools,
community action without touching on
the deceased, self-medication, horses.

As the wheeled coffin slid forward,
the widow stepped from the front pew.
She lowered the tousled brilliance of her hair to the cloth-covered surface,
kissed it, and whispered:

"You are so stupid."

A Refusal to Mutate

Cro-Magnon, mulish, reluctant to alterations,
abstracted by thoughts
of killing the gentle Neanderthals
as they daubed on anthracite walls
with exquisite care,
taking their caves,
jumping up and down on their fires.

Impassioned by Real Estate,
they would have gone mad with rapture
had they foreseen bombs, Uzis, napalm.
Still —
one arrow would suffice,
for now.

With the deliciousness of charred Mammoth, Stone Ox,
burps, farts,
wonderful, grease-smeared fingers,
obesity became a sacrament
unchallenged by Jenny Craig, Hamburger Helper,
Lean Cuisine, Rolaids.

Crazed by the glamour of the rank, gland-searing smell
of never-washed women,
hairy in rancid leopard,
bits of bone ornamenting their tresses,

untouched by Cover Girl, Elle, Clairol, bras,
mascara for exophthalmic eyes —.

The Cro-Magnon, Homo erectus, Liberals, Conservatives, Tories, Sharia
flame out, causing extinction.
(many arrows for fifty billion people)
forever true to 'no change,'
chanting "Kill — Eat — Screw!"

Glamour

Livestock

She could have been the Dairy Princess everyone said,
with her blond curls and those bosoms.
But instead of cutting ribbons at the Zucchini Festival
the pubescent fifteen-year-old ran off with the town degenerate
who lived in an abandoned gas station on his sister's property.

Her policeman father dashed out onto the highway in his pajamas,
shouting, waving his gun,
trying to stop the borderline princess and her fattish forty-five-year-old
consort as they rattled away in the Ford.

For a month, they lived on pizza and beer,
hung out in bars with some drunken Indians who worked the farms,
threw Jack Daniels bottles out the window
while the car crept through sleepy towns near the state border.

At the motorcycle races,
she jumped up and down with glee
as the riders roared off in clouds of dust.
He sat phlegmatically on the roof of the car inert as a toad.

He drove her to all-night house parties deep in the hills
where teenagers threw up in the bushes
after smashing the windows with rocks.
She had never had so much fun!

They were on their way to the tractor pull
when the car coughed and shuddered. He got out, stared at it,
pushed it up against the road shoulder near the cemetery and sighed.

Opening the door, she stepped daintily onto the pavement
her hair bright as a tiara, raising her hand majestically.
Cars slammed to a halt.
Ignoring them, she accepted a ride with a man in a pickup truck
whose tattooed arms rested on the steering wheel.

The End of August

A month when the monotony of summer thick as gas station oil
seeps into the fields
and spectators in the bleachers at the town park
watch the last baseball game hoping for fistfights,
broken noses, the emergency squad.

For the hundredth time,
supper is potato salad, hamburgers, ice cream
and after the baby sitters come for a night
of staring at TV re-runs and last season's movies
leaving the children to terrorize one another upstairs
as long as they don't fight,
the parents depart for some entertainment.

In bars where mounted deer heads
stare over jars of pickled sausages
and strips of toilet paper lie sodden
on the floor of the stopped-up toilets,
women in gold lame stretch pants are dragged languorously
around the dance floor
by men whose sideburns are hairy as caterpillars.

The jukebox throbs out country music like a transplanted heart,
telling it like it is,
and the overweight waitress savors her first gin and ginger ale
of the evening

while somebody's wife makes Cleopatra eyes
at a State Trooper.

The oldest alcoholic in America licks his cigarette
before dropping it into his beer
and falls off the bar stool
as his octogenarian girlfriend grabs for his arm.
The evening fades away
and the bartender heaves a truck driver
through the plate glass window.

Exhausted couples stagger out into the greasy night.
Down the block in their star-lighted bedrooms,
surrounded by broken toys, crumpled bed clothes,
and a spot where the dog vomited,
children, stupefied into an angry sleep, wait for Christmas.

The Pacifist

The idea of aggression maddened the country doctor,
ate into him like acid fuming on pavement.
"I hate violence!" he muttered in his examining room
while massaging Dale Hick's prostate.

Outside, in a waiting room full of strangled coughs,
his American Indian wife, who pretended she was Spanish,
presided at the corner desk.
She was not a nurse.

He reached into his drawer for a stethoscope,
came up with a nest of worm-like pink hair curlers.
Ripping off his shoe, he hurled it through the open door
over the patients' heads.

His wife averted her rusty crow-black hair
as the object smashed the glass of the medical diploma on the wall.
"Next, Clyde Grupp," she announced, slow-hipping her way
across the room
with the patient's records in her hand.

The doctor slammed the door and stared out the window.
"We live in a barbaric society," he explained
to the fourteen-year-old boy
as he jabbed a tetanus shot through the fabric of his jeans.
"When I see violent people — I want to kill them!"

At the desk, his native wife applied mascara with pink tipped fingers.

Blood Line

Duane's great aunt Erline was the Exalted President
of the Library Social Association.
Wearing white gloves, she presided at teas,
and loathed her relatives, especially her niece, Duane's mother,
a large woman slightly flattened on one side where
her breast had encountered a wringer washer.
She'd chased the bull through the pasture once
in heavy black galoshes, wild hair flying,
shouting at the Puerto Ricans who worked the fields.
Duane's father was remote, dreamy, fond of his cows,
preferring to spend long hours in the barn.

When he was twenty-five,
Duane married a pregnant fifteen-year-old with big bosoms,
and they went to live in a cabin in the woods
off the gas company right-of-way,
where he strung lanterns powered by stolen electricity.
They dumped their garbage in the ravine
near the salt licks he set out to lure deer.
There was always a recently killed, bloody animal
strung up to cure in the shed.
He and his wife had several scabby children
who eventually quit school, caused trouble.
His oldest girl took up with the son of the town alcoholic,
and they moved into the chicken coop behind the cabin.

Duane cleaned it up, scraped the chicken droppings off the floor.

The adolescent parents had no jobs but soon had a baby girl named Patsy.
They lay around the place smoking pot, eating potato chips,
watching TV on Duane's second set, raiding his freezer,
cooking ham on an old electric hot plate,
grease spattered all over the floor.
"You've gotta get jobs! Stop hanging around the house all the time!" he
told them.
His daughter huffed. "If you don't like it, we'll give the baby away."

Duane started carrying Patsy around all day, pointing out butterflies
and birds,
took her down to the stand he operated on the main road
near the hotel
selling vegetables from his mother's farm — and live bait.
At three o'clock he closed up and went to the tavern.
Patsy crept on the floor around the bar stools.
He loved the little girl more than anything.
Propping her up on the bar, he gazed into her clear blue eyes
and told the other drinkers:
"She's going to be something some day. Look at those eyes,
and she's got long fingers,
that means she's artistic.
Maybe she'll be a famous painter — or a lawyer.
You better believe it."

Tiffany and Beauty

When she dropped out of the eleventh grade,
her parents set up a little beauty parlor on the corner of the porch
near the coat rack and the winter boots.
There was a sink, beautician's chair and a mirror with movie star lights.
Everyone said she had a real talent since her sister, Alana,
taught her how to make pin curls.

But this week things went wrong.
First, she broke up with her boyfriend,
bare chest, blond hair, black beard, in shorts
torn so his underwear showed.
A twenty-five-year-old who operated a fork lift moving mountains of
dirt all day.

He was mad at her because she wouldn't let him
take their relationship to the next level,
beyond the saliva and the salty fingers and the nudity.
"I'm only sixteen!"
"Don't you love me?"
She was scared because when Alana had gotten pregnant
they made her give the baby away,
and now she cried a lot at night.
He was insistent, and when she wouldn't do it,
he pushed her out of his truck clutching her clothes,
forced to walk home.

Then her steady customer,
Jennifer of the massive hair,

fell asleep under the drier.
She was rolling up Mrs. Pond's meager gray threads
and talking about her boyfriend, when a scorched smell
alerted her, and a lot of burnt stuff had to be cut off
leaving Jennifer's head looking lopsided.

The next day, when she bleached Angie Pasquale's dark, Italian hair,
she had to use very strong stuff and the fumes made her eyes water,
but the color only got down to red.
"Do it again!" Angie insisted. "I want to go blond!"
"I don't know if that's a good idea."
She mixed another awful batch,
rolled up the curlers and put her under the drier in a green plastic cap,
left her under for an extra fifteen minutes just to be sure.
When she took the cap off, the curlers stuck to it, falling onto the floor
like pink worms covered with something gluey.
"My hair!" Angie shrieked.
"I didn't want to do it!"

Angie was talked out of a lawsuit
when Tiffany promised to clean her house every week for a year,
and the client left after dubious glances in the mirror at her brush cut.
Then, Mr. Casketti called from the funeral home
to ask if she wanted a job styling hair on the deceased.
"They don't give you any trouble," he explained.

Instead, she called up and enrolled in the Pandora School of Modeling.
Be a Model and earn Big Money the phone book ad said.
After all, she thought, I am an attractive girl.

Anniversary

Hours after he watched her shadow slide under the door
he caught up with her in a bar
where she was chatting up a State Trooper: she loved uniforms,
he was a brutish-looking guy — she liked that too.
"Go home! You're tired!" she told him,
but he made his beer last three hours
until the cop gave up, the drunks wandered off
and the place closed into a powdery darkness.
The weekends were all like that now.

On this pale, dust-washed Sunday afternoon
he drove up the hill and parked off the road,
watching the hawks sweep the sky over the valley
and knew that he would kill her.
He remembered their wedding.
She, so perfect in her lace and veils
yet at the reception carrying a stuffed animal
pretending to make it talk.
They had to dance with it pressed between them.
She clutched it in the car when they left for the honeymoon
screaming out the window at the guests:
"Peanut Brittle! Say goodbye! goodbye!"
waving its dopey arm and twisting its head.

And six years of high jinks with the people they ran around with,
flirting with the men,
daring one man "dance with me"
her red nails like blood flowers on his back

while their pelvises clanked
and then buying him an expensive camera
with her entire paycheck.
She loved black, black jeans,
tight dresses that exposed her breasts,
highlighted her bleached skin.

There were no children.

He didn't know if he'd wanted them.
She took up so much of his time
that there was never room for much else.
The hawks were far away now,
always two — they mate for life.

The hills blurred as he started the truck
for the drive to his brother's house
where his shotgun slept in the rafters of the garage.

Glamour

She was fifteen when she met this wild, delusional bad boy
eyes like fractured coke bottles and a double ridge of muscle
near his spine, six-foot-four.
She rode on the back of his motorcycle — "hog" he called it,
her face pressed into the snake tattoos on his shoulder
listening to the music of the wind.

They went to a motorcycle blessing in a scuffed farmer's field
the air hot with hay and manure,
a field jammed with bikes gunned by men in cut-off vests,
helmets adorned with flags, crosses, club emblems,
men accompanied by straw-haired blondes.
A stoned-looking priest performed the benediction.

Later in that marvelous summer there were tractor pulls,
motocross races,
and an auction barn selling cows, sheep, boxes of junk,
turquoise jewelry, kittens and Amish cheeses.
Everything smelled of melted ice cream, sweat and insecticide.
Always there were fistfights, a tense, wary circling
until the scene turned purple and black
with noses broken, the crowd pulling back
frightened and fascinated.

She became his old lady but they never married.
They rented a ramshackle farmhouse
and nailed signs to the trees:
No cars, trucks or horses allowed in the driveway.

There was a wood stove for heat
but it never got above fifty in the winter.
Beyond the kitchen window was an orchard
where blossoms exploded in the spring
and raccoons shrieked at night.
Every fall she canned the apples he picked for her.

He named the children after western outlaws:
William Bonney, Jesse James, Clyde Barrow, Bonnie Parker.
and taught them to hold on to the back of the cycle
when they were babies as he bumped gently around the yard.
All those children scattered,
but they didn't turn out too bad.

Now, he sits at the end of the thick bar, that years ago
he yanked off its base during a fight
and shattered the mirror with a bottle
while the bartender cowered on the floor.
He's shrunk.
His shoulders are little knobs,
and the beer glass trembles in his hand,
the bike sits dusty in the shed.
He can't ride anymore, liver, the doctor said.
Well, he'd earned it.
But he still has those green eyes.
She pats his fading tattoos. Yes, she'd do it again.

The Little Toad

Early in Rhonda's pregnancy
she shoveled a mountain of pea gravel in the driveway and
threw herself down the front steps of her trailer.
The only nourishment she could keep down
was beer.
She sat on the couch, swallowing foam, watching TV
her feet on a case of Budweiser
auxiliary cases stacked near the door
but nothing worked.
The baby arrived after a twenty-hour labor.

Rhonda called the child the toad,
propped her up on a bed with a bottle while she gossiped on the phone
with friends.
Evenings the baby was left alone in her crib
staring into the envelope of night
while her mother went out to the stock car races, beer blasts.
The toad was neglected so much that the neighbors called the
Child Protection Agency.
After that, Rhonda brought her in a carry-cart to the gin mills,
parked the baby under a bar stool or on a table in a booth,
beer fumes forming a halo around her head.

When the toad was six months old
Rhonda took her to the mall,
dried oatmeal crusted on her dirty clothes, hair matted
but still breathtakingly beautiful through the grime.

A woman wanted to kiss her.
"That's the most exquisite child I've ever seen.
She looks like Elizabeth Taylor — that black hair-those violet eyes."

A man offered Rhonda his card. "Fairfield Modeling Agency."
"This beautiful child would be perfect for our ad campaign.
Don't worry about her clothes," he sniffed. "We'll dress her."

She took the toad to the modeling studio and watched the baby
being posed and lighted, in a pink dress, smelling of soap, her hair curled,
clapping her chubby hands at the caressing eye of the camera.

As Rhonda signed the studio contract, the owner told her,
"You must put the child's name down.
Her picture will be in magazines all over the country.
She'll become famous as the Fairfield Baby."
Rhonda thought a minute, stared reflectively at this radiant infant
whose real name she couldn't remember.
"Elizabeth," she said. "Her name is Elizabeth."

Procession

The Pritchetts rode horses one brilliant summer
in the Fourth of July Parade,
buttermilk tails flicking dust over people in webbed lawn chairs
along the road, and clopped, swaying, high above the crowd,
between the Silver Prince Drum Corps and a 4-H troop.
No banner was as bright and arrogant as this family.

They mismanaged their farm,
ignoring the hired hands who smashed tavern windows
with bar stools
fell drunkenly off tractors and lay vomiting in ditches
while the cows stood up to their knees in manure in the barn
next to a cache of CD's and tapes
that the girls had boosted from Record Shack.

The parents gave parties where guests
pulled the hostess's dress down
and sprayed her snowy Alps with whipped cream
as her husband French-kissed her best friend in the kitchen.
The children watched from the stair landing
waiting for sirens, fistfights.

The fourteen-year-old drove her parents SUV
into the front of a house on the main road and gazed in surprise
through a window wreathed in broccoli and lettuce
at the family cowering over their roast beef dinner.

The oldest boy carried a shotgun onto the school bus
wrapped in newspaper
hoping to shoot his Social Studies teacher.

Barmaids, car salesmen and tumescent neighbors
invaded the wreckage of their nights,
while the parties get louder and the drinks stronger,
time gutted their solipsistic beauty.
The divorce was not pretty.

A second boy perished in a motorcycle accident at twenty-two.
His sister wore gold sandals and a heliotrope satin blouse
at his wake.
The following spring she was shot to death
outside a Nevada casino.
The other children married, separated, started repair shops, got fat.

Now, no one remembers that lambent summer
when in boots and fringes, turquoise and silver,
taller than mortals,
they rode horses in the Fourth of July parade.

Procession II

She sat astride a large, warm horse at the rear of the parade
behind the Junior Farmers' gilded livestock wagon
in front of an ambulance with Pennsylvania dealer's plates
and wished that her hangover would go away

Her sister, shoulders like a quarterback,
made obscene gestures at her from the curb
and pretended to puke
but it didn't cheer her.

Earlier that summer, her mother spent frenzied weeks
canning beans,
stacking hundreds of jars on shelves in the side porch,
the kitchen filled with baskets and steam
and in August, at the Corn Festival, hit on a guy
in the beer tent, her face urgent.
She wore a short raincoat although it was a hot night, bare legs,
dark circles under her eyes, talking, talking, waving a cigarette.

The man came to the house next Friday
stood on the porch.
"She's a married woman! Get out!"

But her mother primped and lipsticked
piled on bracelets like a Spanish dancer,
sidled past, her perfume gagging the air,
came in at four a.m. rumpled and smeared.

Their father, silent and white, wouldn't talk to the girls.

A month later their mother disappeared with the man,
he had four children — a wife.
There was no note.

If she hadn't gotten pneumonia when she was ten
and they went to Florida to recover,
her mother picking up a seventeen-year-old hitchhiker
on the way home,
letting him stay in the house for three months —
if she hadn't flunked geometry, broken her leg in a bike accident —

The night before the Labor Day Parade, she and her sister
drank a bottle of Thunderbird
went outside and threw the beans all over the lawn
smashed the jars in the driveway.
It didn't help.

Now, flags were being hoisted, the horse snorted strings of foam,
the Junior Farmers stopped combing their fat animals,
town politicians revved up a convertible
tossing handfuls of candy to the crowd.
The parade lurched forward.

Round and Round

Darlene met Roy at McGonigles Moonlight Tavern one Saturday night
when she and her girlfriends were out for a good time.
She liked his blond hair and his chubby, if somewhat blurred face.
He impressed her by memorizing her telephone number
and calling her the very next day.

They dated for six months and then decided to get married.
A local wedding was out because his wife refused to give him a divorce
and on a sour day in March,
they drove to Pennsylvania and exchanged vows
before a befuddled judge.
She was Mrs. Roy Crumper, more or less.

Darlene had been wed before, briefly, the ceremony performed
next to her hospital bed the day the baby was born,
the new husband momentarily captivated by the adorable little girl.
It didn't last, but the divorce was legal.

Roy and his somewhat-married wife bought a trailer
and gave loud parties every weekend with the walls pulsating
the tape deck turned up to frantic —
while Darlene's baby fussed unnoticed in the tiny back room.
They held a contest to see how many people
could be crammed into the narrow structure
because her mother said that it looked small.
Thirty and a keg of beer was the limit.

Sex had always made her nervous
and Roy certainly didn't rattle her teeth
but he didn't know that until later,
and anyway he preferred drinking
and spent many nights lying spread-eagled
on their minuscule front lawn
next to the plaster gnomes she preferred to grass.

Darlene's main ambition was to be in the beauty business, and
she found employment at Vanessa's Magic Nails.
The first day at work she was terribly nervous.
She brought a bottle of Four Roses,
stashing it in the store room with the beauty supplies.
"I'm not going to touch it," she told Vanessa.
"Just so I know its there."
Her job was soaking and doing cuticles, until she was experienced
enough for polishing and painting little stars and initials.

Roy was the nicest guy in the world when he wasn't drinking
but through the years those times became rare.
He and Darlene fought all the time,
and finally he got in his pickup truck and drifted away.
He wasn't missed.

Her daughter finished high school, joined the Army,
and her mother passed away.
She paid up the trailer with the small inheritance.
Magic Nails had begun to bore her.

She was sick of painting petal pink, siren red and hot tamale
over and over day after day.
When Vanessa insisted that she execute American flags and goldfish
on the customer's nails — she quit.

Now, every afternoon at four,
she dresses carefully in open- toed high heels,
hair in a shellacked upsweep,
walks precariously from Lou's Mobile Home Court down the highway,
breasts swinging like a pendulum in her pink crepe blouse
as she enters McGonigles.

All evening, she sits delicately on a bar stool,
cradling a succession of gin and tonics,
talking with the regulars, laughing at their jokes, dancing with them.
She gazes at her reflection mirrored behind the rows of shiny bottles
and thinks about how happy she is.

Night Sounds

He's listening
from the bedroom
across the layers of his brother's troubled breathing.
Down the hall, she's in the kitchen,
a gin and tonic on the dinner-stained table, murmuring into the CB radio,
talking to truckers while their rigs hurtle through the invitational night
to park under the heavy trees.

She never brings them into the house
but, crushing her purple-tipped cigarette,
slips out the door barefoot
onto the grass.

His dead father's shotgun hangs in the attic of his mind.
He tried to use it once
took it loaded from the front closet,
aimed at the truck luminous in the moonlight
but, shaken, powerless,
could only run into the field, crying.

She'll come in the house in an hour
padding softly
surrounded by fireflies,
past his room thick with pain
to her bed
for another night.

Heaven's Tourists

They appeared one spring
when the air was full of whistling blackbirds
to occupy a desolate cabin down near the ravine
with no water or toilet.
The woman, hair on her legs as thick as an animals
clutched a religious object embellished with fake rubies.
Her unshaven husband was ferret-eyed.
They wandered the roads muttering garbled bible verses,
and their little boy did not go to school or speak to anyone.
We heard that they had been to South America,
where she shouted liturgical invectives at the bewildered natives,
while the jungle heaved and pulsated with jaguars and cawing birds.
We heard that they had been expelled from the
Cattaraugus Reservation
by hostile Indians who did not want to be saved.
At the cabin, she set up a loudspeaker
and blasted the words of her sermons into the woods
all night long, scaring the owls,
until a police car crept down the dirt road.
They were aggressive, these holy healers,
kicking at snapping dogs, banging on doors clamped shut by people
trapped in their kitchens.
They stuffed the mailboxes with misspelled pamphlets about hellfire
that the wind scattered over the fields like bits of lace.
He probed the empty space in his mouth after
smashing his upper plate with a hammer
and waited for the lord to send him a new set of teeth,
waited while he shot at animals near the stream.

She boiled the carcasses into violent stews.
Then, suddenly as an erased shadow,
they were gone.
The front door of the cabin swung loosely,
an exploded bag of gagbage leaked smears of food
onto the dirt path, savaged by wasps.
Neighbors opened their windows to the moist summer air
and went outdoors, giddy with freedom.
After a while, the birds came back.

The Fireman

Caved-in rafters over rotting hay in a barn far in the hills.
He had prowled here many nights
listening to the owls and nighthawks whooshing to the ground,
the car hidden under the trees black as a shadow.
Tonight he walked to the structure as it creaked with the wind
forced the crusted door and materialized inside like a ghost.
Kneeling near decayed manure the consistency of ashes
he carefully built a paper shrine, touched it with a tiny flame.
For a moment he stared at the photographic light
slowly developing against the slatted walls
then stumbled out into the barnyard
the hot tissue of his lungs exploding
before he careened down the hill to the station house,
anticipating the siren about to flood the valley with shrieks,
where the ceremonial truck gleamed in the anthracite night.

Waiting for Spring

She watched,
thin with hate,
from the frost-rimmed window
as the game warden heaved the bloody deer carcass
out of his pickup truck into the ringing air —
road kill.

Her husband, plaid shirt, ear-muffed hat,
fired up the tractor down near the barn
waiting to drag the animal
into the woods
where the coyotes howled.
It had been a tough winter.

Inside,
the wood stove popped.
It was fifty degrees in the farmhouse.
There was no hot water,
dishes froze in the sink at night.

Two years ago,
they lived in an apartment complex in town
with utilities, security.
She remembered taking his t-shirts out of the drier,
kissing their warm surface before folding them.
She loved him then.

Now these shirts hang stiffly frozen
on the backyard clothesline.
When his father died and left a little money,
her husband read Mother Earth Magazines, books on survival skills.
Wanted to subsist on the land, grow their food.
"Off the grid" he extolled as he sold her car and bought the tractor,
purchased an old wrecked farm house on a hill
that had been on the market for years.

The garden was full of weedy undersized produce that
she canned in the fall on a propane stove
but was afraid to eat
as white mold sent its fingers into the jars.
She hated to go into the fields,
fearful of foxes, skunks, raccoons.
Bats infested the barn.

When their chickens died of viruses and worms,
he bought a cow
who stood in manure in the barn
bawling to be milked.
They took the milk to the co-op
but it was not certifiable,
had to be dumped onto the compost pile,
thin white streaks bluing the dirt.

"Hogs!" he said:
"That's where the market is!
Next spring we'll sell the cow and buy hogs."

She pictured them —
obese, lying in filthy straw
covered with flies.

She wanted her car back —
or a furnace.

The night after the deer carcass came,
the huge sycamore tree darkening the kitchen window
roared, split apart and fell broken into the yard.
In the morning,
the room was full of brilliant light.
Marveling at the sun gleaming on the shabby counters,
the cracked linoleum,
she gently touched the pine table, hugging herself.

"Firewood! It'll last the winter," he said,
pulling on his crusty jacket as he went to the barn
to get the chain saw.

She ran to the bedroom,
stuffed her clothes into paper bags, lipstick, bras,
her grandmother's cameos.
Lurched down the blood-streaked driveway
snow piling over the tops of her boots, chilling her ankles,
out into the road
where far below in the valley
the village glittered in the sunlight.

Talisman

Under a smoking moon,
fire broke open the roof
and caved the sky in on their bed
before the trucks came.
Men in rubber coats dragged hoses through the mud
and trampled the porch
where everything was ruined.

He and his wife moved into a trailer back beside the barn.
They'd walk around the pond, feed the Canada Geese,
play cards every evening.
She never spoke after the fire
but sat in the window
staring at a sky full of tumultuous birds.

Once a week, he goes to the house,
pulls open the the stuck, blistered door.
On the kitchen table, heat-broken canning jars
spill plums touched with a filigree of mold.
Water-stained boxes and clothes lie tangled in the hallway.

In the living room,
beyond the charred couch and smashed lamps,
a dressmaker's dummy wears the blouse she was sewing.
Carefully, he touches the stiff silk
unmindful of the soot that comes off on his hand.

Starstruck

She's seated on a bar stool at Norm's Tavern
down near the creek
under a sky saturated with stars
sipping port wine while the red beer sign throbs.

He didn't come with her.
He's at the house staring out the window
at the moon-faced cattle near the stone barn,
and at the TV sets, refrigerators and maimed farm machinery
strewn on the lawn,
patting the iridescent fish heads nailed to the porch wall,
clearing his throat.

She doesn't mind living in a valley where snowplows fall
into the ditches in winter
and there are no stores on the corner or anywhere —
just mountain-high hills, hawks, barns with hex signs,
motorcycle gangs.

The juke box is playing 'Crazy'
and she remembers other nights — being driven off the road
by two men in a pickup truck
with a German Shepherd snarling in the back.
She remembers feeling yellow with fright after being
knocked to the ground
in a restaurant parking lot
and being kicked.

But she loves the blackened house, wrecked outbuildings,
spooked horses,
the comforting litter and decay.
Another glass of wine and she'll go home.
Chickens will have wandered through a forgotten door,
feathered dowagers squatting on the couch.
He'll be in bed,
moonlight streaking his face in the soft night.

Summer Kisses

In the fried-popcorn air of July,
surrounded by people eating sausage subs, sugar waffles,
corn dogs,
pushing chocolate-smeared babies in strollers,
Debbie wandered through the County Fairgrounds in tight jeans
looking for thrills.

She had assured her mother,
who wanted her to be an elementary teacher
and be dull — dull — dull forever,
that she was baby-sitting for a neighbor.

At the Tilt-a-Whirl, the attendant's eyes lingered
on her gold navel ring as he asked
in a voice as seductive as a train whistle at midnight:
"Want a ride? You don't need no ticket."

She rode three times,
flipping up into the burning sky over the concession stands,
the carousel,
until her stomach heaved
and the hot dog and soda rose in her throat.

The next day, she returned, wearing a low-cut blouse
that exposed a buttterfly tattoo her mother didn't know about.
His hand cupped her shorts
as he assisted her into the ride.

She spun dizzily all afternoon sending him provocative glances.

That evening, he led her down a dark path
past the Stars of Tomorrow Pavilion,
to an empty storage shed
behind the Indian Village dance ceremony,
embraced her on a pile of horse blankets
to the throb of drums and the slap of moccasins.

"Come with me," he purred. "You're so pretty.
I bet you could be a star in one of the grandstand stage acts."
She saw herself in spangles, cheeks showing,
wearing movie star makeup,
astride a panting horse high above the crowd.

They crossed the state in the carnival's railroad car —
no air conditioning —
traveling from one county fair to the next,
caught up in the hurly-burly atmosphere, the side shows,
games of chance.
She was fascinated by his blond sideburns and alluring blue eues.

But her job consisted of shoveling enormous mounds of
Clydesdale manure from the barns,
selling tickets near the parking lot in a sweltering booth
wreathed in gasoline fumes
and flagging cars,
as she watched the excitement of the midway with angry eyes.

Girls in provocative outfits loitered near the Tilt-a-Whirl.

A volcanic blond posed against the ride,
her arm around the attendant's waist,
cranberry lips teasing his earlobes.

The cramped railway car pulsed with shouts and accusations
as it lurched through the fields of frothing corn stalks
heading for Albany
where the same crews assembled the concessions
and identical barns held 4-H kids, obese hogs and flies.

One afternoon in late August,
she fell into her mother's door,
jeans filthy, her neck purple with fading hickeys,
clutching a soiled pink teddy bear,
Her only souvenir of the summer.

Saturday Morning

After speeding through the blackened night
chased by vigilantes, angry spouses, girlfriends
and the fire department,
after burning up the back roads
and dodging knockout punches in bars,
the town residents fell into unconscious beds
before the morning sun bleached out their desires.

Near the General Store, a puzzled husband
stares at the hole in his dining room
where he fired his shotgun through the ceiling at his wife
cowering upstairs.
He's sure she's been cheating.
"Vera — Vera —"
he calls to the empty rooms,
kicking at a pile of broken plaster.

A mile away,
lying on her couch,
a woman wakes to smashed furniture, ripped drapes and the dog
lapping a pool of beer.
Her sixteen-year-old's birthday party
has been a success.
Thank God the State Police didn't come this time.
Sick as a bruise, she closes her eyes as the room rocks.

An obese woman eats jelly donuts and drinks coffee
at a newspaper covered table
in a gas station on the main road
before heaving herself ponderously out to service the pumps.
Her husband snores in his Lazy Boy near the TV.
He won forty dollars at euchre last night.
Her disturbed son
leaves quietly for his compulsive twenty mile walk
murmuring softly.

The Justice of the peace places a bottle of Four Roses
in a special holster near shift of his car so he can drink
while he drives and roars off,
his deer rifle bouncing on the back seat.

In a farmhouse on Snake Creek Road
a youth slides a pile of magazines illustrated with pictures of men
posing in scanty thongs, their coiled muscles gleaming,
under his salty bed and hopes his mother won't clean there.
His antenna, delicate as a butterfly, senses the hired man
forking hay in the barn.

High on a hill,
the town curiosity stands naked and scratching
before a picture window,
wreathed in smoke from the fireplace
where piles of Goodwill clothes
smolder more cheaply than firewood.

His housemate and dearest friend, his horse,
gazes fondly over his shoulder at the panoramic valley below.
A drunk nods blissfully in his locked car
in front of Chet's Night Owl Tavern.
Firemen joyously hose down their trucks,
hawks wheel and churn the air
as light glistens on the headstones in the cemetery.

The Sweet Life

Breakwall

In the strawberry-scented
day we crossed the beach
near poppies and irises piled on the grass
and walked out onto the narrow stone ledge
carrying a steaming pot, teacups,
tiny sandwiches of spiced ham, cupcakes full of walnuts.

Seated on the cloth precariously, far out
beyond the sailboats and cruisers pinned against the harbor,
we laughed,
dropped bits of egg salad to the crowding fish,
mayonnaise smearing their nacreous skin.
The breakers drenched us with fragrant spray
near boulders streaming with seaweed.
The provocative horizon was endless, creamy, pink, full of summer hawks.
Nothing could touch us.

Later, as the years pressed into a scrapbook,
living in houses where secrets slid through the walls like spiders
and costumes and masks lay piled in the attic,
we ate burnt toast beside sealed windows,
gazed into tarnished mirrors.

Driving from the darkened city past shells of factories,
boat hulls stiff in the oily canal,
we walked from the fractured shore out onto the breakwall,
our feet slipping as crystals formed on our faces like patches of frostbite.

We slid to a halt, stumbled, spilling the tepid tea, shattering the cups.

Gouts of water sluiced our hair
coating it with a thousand icicles.

We struggled to raise numb arms toward each other to embrace
but we were frozen creatures
sheathed in ice
unable to touch.

Happy Marriage

Willard collected
magenta plastic Christmas trees, dented coffee pots, shoes
rubbed to a powdery brown, truncated golf clubs, wheel-less
bicycle frames.
Driven to a state of rapture by garage sales, flea markets,
country auctions, the quarterly town trash pickup,
he gloated orgiastically over boxes and boxes of things he could carry
home, push into the crammed garage,
the packed cellar, hoist onto the drier along with a cracked bird bath,
mildewed lawn furniture, buckled suitcases spilling discolored
underwear.
In his suffocating living room, where he occupied the couch
along with a torn economy-size Cheetos package,
mold-etched crackers, half-eaten salami sandwiches,
his eyes caressed a ravished taxidermist's raccoon,
a broken laser printer,
his hand lovingly stroked a rusted bicycle pump.

Shirley didn't mind his collection at all.
She collected men.
The UPS driver hunched over a packing box,
the side-burned teenager pumping her gas,
a pudgy Chinese waiter at the Pagoda House
"LoMein? Fortune cookie? You want?"
The mailman inserting letters,
the butcher guarding sausages and meat loaf at the deli, "Next!"
A uniformed cop who arrested her, siren blaring, for rash driving.

Willard and Shirley went out together Saturday nights
to a grimy tavern on the main road.
His eyes eagerly scanned the Hershey bar dispenser,
the live- bait vending machine.
At the bar, he secreted swizzle sticks, napkins,
palmed shot glasses and beer nuts,
ketchup-stained paper plates.

She lowered her cleavage to the bartender,
crossing her legs provocatively for the truck driver on the adjacent stool,
while slipping her phone number to the bus boy.

Toward the end of the evening
she disappeared for an hour or two,
emerging joyous, rumpled, with lipstick-smeared teeth
from the cab of a semi.
His pockets were gorged with empty bottles, martini glasses,
an old baseball cap he found in the men's room.

As they contentedly rode home, her hand patting his knee, she asked:
"Did you have a good evening?"

Noel, Noel

Hermione, grand dame of the tiny hamlet,
penned her annual Christmas letter
at a polished mahogany desk,
tapes of carols softly playing,
the old traditional ones,
Adeste Fidelis, O Little Town of Bethlehem,
while on the roof
against the purplish sky
her asthmatic husband,
blood pressure bursting,
attached a silver sleigh full of wrapped packages
in understated blue and white
before twining velvet ribbons around the columns of the front porch.

Each person in the village received the long letter
full of Hermione's righteous observations,
her views on that state of the world

"Spontaneous giving must be organized!" it commanded.

The Callahans, secure in their snowmobile, shotguns and beer world,
amidst a yard strewn with plastic Bambis, inedible gingerbread man,
flashing lights, grinning elves,
erected two huge, illuminated Santas
that undulated and bellowed in the fluorescent night. HO-HO-HO.
The Christmas missive was trampled in the driveway.

"Abstinence is the moral responsibility of the entire community."

Her unmarried daughter
in her greasy apartment over the gas station,
where outside garbage cans were piled in the kitchen
full of putrid eggs and coffee grounds
next to the cat's overflowing litter box
used the letter as a place mat for her cereal-encrusted table

where the baby chewed a large chunk out of it.

"Capital punishment is a must in a civilized society."

High above an automobile junkyard,
in a blackened house full of chickens and dogs
filthy with hardened manure,
dense with animal hair,
her disinherited brother
opened a beer bottle with his teeth
and used the publication
to cover up the collie's vomit.

"The borders must be closed to immigration."

Her cleaning woman
in a cozy trailer down near the creek
blissfully listening to *Grandma Got Run Over By a Reindeer*
on her dinette radio, while watching Judge Judy on TV chuckled:

"It must be that time of year again,"
and used the paper to train the new puppy.
who promptly blessed it.

"University entrance exams must be made more difficult! Only
students who are college material should be allowed to attend."

The volunteer firemen,
watching X-rated movies in a locked upstairs room of the firehouse
as they waited for a conflagration call,
stacked the pamphlets in the wood stove
as if the atmosphere wasn't hot enough.

As Hermione presided over her sterling silver tea service
in her exquisitely tasteful living room
and passed tiny cranberry turnovers
to the Ladies of the Church Auxiliary,
women heavy with violet hair and breeding,
she reminded them:

"It is my duty, you see.
Someone must be the standard bearer."

Tarnished Glass

——*Gene*

Gene dreamed of a woman
in a special apron soft with flour,
tart with the smell of cinnamon,
a house warmed by the heat of pies
fragrant with lemon.

In August, he collected his elderly aunt
from the Home and Creative Arts Building at the County Fair —
a place chattering with artificial flowers, doilies,
piles of double wedding ring quilts.
Behind a shelf lush with canned preserves
he saw her, long black hair, innocent green eyes.
Magnetized,
he touched the jars lovingly.
"Did you can these? And these?
You won the ribbons?"
"Yes. Yes.
My name is Renee."
He fantasized spiced peaches, succulent cherries, plump blueberries,
sweet pears.

For six months she cooked.
London Broil, Brioches with Salmon, Chicken Divan,
Pork Roast with Prunes.
She was a secretary.

She would quit her job, of course.

For their wedding reception, Luigi's Italian Gardens,
Renee made the ushers' boutonnieres, the bridesmaids' bouquets,
center pieces of heather and daisies.
They lived in a log style home
high on a hill surrounded by evergreens.
Hawks, jays, crows, whirled and spun in the glittering air.

The months drifted.
Renee filled the bird feeders, put apples out for the deer.
She cooked less frequently.
pizza studded with acid green olives appeared one evening
then tacos, chicken wings,
Chinese take-out replaced spiced peaches.
She seemed a stranger to domestic machines.

Gene took to staring at the birds
falling like omens through the pines.

"What did you do today?" tentatively.
"I walked in the woods. It was beautiful.
I saw a Coopers Hawk and a fox."
"Shouldn't the Christmas tree needles be vacuumed? It's almost March."
"Tomorrow." she smiled.

The days blackened as the house became more toxic.
The living room was a voyage through discordant booby traps
of clothes, papers, garden implements.

His anger coagulated in the kitchen

above a sink full of dishes
half-drowned in brown water stirring with maggots.

He grabbed the abandoned vacuum and
hurled it across the room
where it lay smashed against the refrigerator
like a truncated insect
startling Renee, reading a paperback novel.

"I don't understand!" he shouted.
"Why the mess! the take-out food? What do you do all day?
I thought you enjoyed homemaking!"
"But what's wrong?" her eyes widened.
"Wrong?"
"You hate me."
"No, no. I love you. I'll always love you. But this filth!
I can't stand it!"

In the cold yellow morning
all of her, make-up, clothes, magazines
vanished.

Gene searched for her
haunted by the possibility of cinnamon,
interrogated her friends.

He never found her.

——*Bobby*

She sat at the end of the bar
under a florescent bloom of country music, loud voices, Budweiser fumes,
nursing a gin and tonic the long evening,
smiling at Bobby
as he slapped down foaming steins of beer, dissected lemons.
Guys watching the football game
strutted by her, hitched their pants, tightened their belts.
During lulls,
Bobby and Renee would whisper together,
his beefy face rapt,
near his trophy, beautiful Renee.
She was there three nights a week and Sundays.

Late at night, after the bar closed
they danced slowly to songs.
"I don't want to wait a million years." — "I'll be your baby,"
her black hair spread over his shoulder in the darkened room,
the little colored lights of the juke box
blinking off and on.
He drove her home through the hyacinth night.

She worked at a veterinary clinic.
She loved animals.

He wanted to marry her, but she put him off.
"Not now."
He persuaded her to move in with him.

She brought Peace Lilies, gardenias, pots of roses,
Boston Ferns to the apartment,
the window sills full, the air perfumed.

She joined a bridge club.
"Bridge? Why not pinochle? We could play together."
"But I always wanted to learn bridge. You could learn. I'll teach you,"
He knew that he couldn't.

She was gone to her card games two nights a week.
"I missed you at the bar. Are you coming Sunday?"
"Oh yes."

Then she became a member of a foreign film group.
Sub- titles, Spanish, sometimes German or Indian,
meeting at an art theater in the city, ten miles away.
"Come to the movie with me."
He tried it.

The theater was cold, seats of hard rotted leather.
A Spanish film about transvestite prostitutes.
He was nauseated.
Her friends drank strange coffees in the lobby,
talked excitedly about the film:
"So astute, and the casting, but the hubris?"
He hated them.

The bar became chaotic.
He argued with the customers,

brooded, staring at Renee's empty seat
as he sneaked shots of whiskey.

She left him a note one evening while he was working.
"I'll always think of you."

The next night, he was injured breaking up a fight,
a beer glass smashed against his jaw, blood running down his shirt,
bottles shattered against the back mirror.
He wanted to wreck faces
turn noses to pulp.

After that, he quit,
started working at another tavern farther out from town
where no one knew him.
Threw all the plants away.

——*Frank*

He loved to kiss her,
lips moving softly,
in the theater, at parties, football games,
surrounded by dancing, martinis, explosive fans,
plates of stuffed mushrooms.
He would stare with enchantment at Renee,

Eventually, they would drive to a meadow
high in the star-lit hills
and she gazed over his shoulder at the lover's moon
the grass damp, the air plangent.

In his town house,
modern, Chinese red door, black floor, white furniture
they discussed marriage, arrangements.
He was a banker.
He didn't want her to have a job.

"But what will I do all day?"
"Oh, hobbies, something."
"I'll weave. I studied textiles once."
She collected beach pebbles on walks
along a stormy shore
listening to pounding waves.
A large loom soon dominated the corner of the living room.

The walls blossomed with intricate hangings made of feathers,
fragments of glass, stones, cloth strips.

He came home every day for lunch.
She was fascinated by his teeth,
running her finger over the interesting crooked bottom surfaces,
the top ones were perfect,
his head thrown back,
fingers stroking her shoulders.

She began to have abdominal pains, doubling over
on the white couch, clutching a hot water bottle.
"The doctor says it's an intestinal problem
"You have medication?"
"Oh, yes."

Then her periods lengthened,
slowly consuming the entire month
except for a few days.
She was tired, disoriented."

He entered the house hopefully
wearing a glittering smile, his eyes glassy.
"Maybe I should have iron shots," she whispered.
He opened his mouth
to reveal the seductive teeth,
but she had fallen asleep.

Vitamin pills littered the kitchen counter,
medical journals were stacked on the coffee table.
Her doctor was mystified.
She slept in flannel pajamas, booties, a little cap that tied under her chin.

He got drunk in the dining room, night after night.

Sores grew on her fever-bleached lips.
The medication was changed, and changed.
New doctors were consulted.

Finally, he drove her to a clinic in another state.
Phone calls and letters filled the air like passenger pigeons.

She checked out of her room two weeks later,
left no forwarding address.

Black Horses

Under the dripping trees, near disordered creeks,
the horses stood in a saturated field,
their dichromatic eyes recording the car speeding near the pasture.
The driver did not notice their sleekness, musculature, the tails freighted
by the cascading downpour.

She was talking excitedly on her CB radio to a trucker.
"I'm getting married! Me and the kids won't have to live with my
mother anymore. Oh, yes, she'll be glad to see us go.
All she does is complain about her varicose legs, baby sitting, my job.
And he's buying us a double wide in the Three Pines Trailer Court.
He gives me anything I want,
roses on my birthday, one for every year."

She turned up the windshield wipers,
their streaks exposing the morbid farms.
The car slid slightly on an oily curve.

"I've had bad relationships, but never got married.
Ma hated my having the two kids.
Amber's father was a drunk
and Randolph's ran a fork lift. I don't see him anymore.
No child support."

The ditches were filling,
shot with yellow silt.
The car fishtailed on the dark pavement.

"Well, I met him on fish fry night, Friday,
at the bar where I'm a waitress.
He's been married before, his wife cheated on him.
No kids —
but he's good to mine,
keeps them in line."

The horses crowded closer together, dark blots against the hills,
exhaling nervously
in the prematurely dark afternoon.

"We've been dating for six months.
I never thought I'd find the right one.
His only flaw is
he sometimes drinks a little too much.
My best friend, Louanne, gave me a shower,
lots of dishtowels and nightgowns. Mostly Coral, that's my color."

Blind to everything but her shining new life
she turned up the steep hill road
driving very fast
and skidded in front of a sedan.
Inside were four women returning from Bingo,
a grandmother, her niece, two neighbors,
talking excitedly about their winnings.
The collision severed the car and shattered the sedan.
When the paramedics found the carnage strewn in the mud
they pried open the door of the wreckage

where the CB was still transmitting the trucker's voice
into the volcanic air.

The horses lifted their heads,
feeling the concussion beneath their delicate hooves.
They broke into a run, then a gallop,
the silvery raindrops glistening on their backs
like splintered light.

The Country People

The Stanleys adored their recently purchased house in the country.
It was worth the forty-five minute drive in the winter
through ten-foot tunnels of banked snow,
miles from their jobs, concerts, lectures, restaurants.
It was their first year.
That summer, they brushed their teeth with bottled water
when the well went dry,
called the honey dipper men to unplug the clogged septic tank,
a plumber to replace the cracked tiles of the leach bed.
Mister Stanley mowed the lawn swathed in respirators and scarves
in deference to his grass allergy.
The rabbits ate their tomatoes,
deer devoured the expensive shrubs that Landscapers Deluxe
had planted at an exorbitant price.
On a night when her husband was at a meeting,
Mrs. Stanley locked herself in the bathroom frozen with fear amid
the creaks, whisperings, cracklings of a settling house.
For Halloween, they gave the trick or treaters five dollars each
because they had neglected to buy candy.
At Christmas, they tied bottles of whiskey to their mailbox
down on the road
as a token of appreciation for the garbage men.
There were rats in the compost pile, squirrels in the attic,
all night, feral cats howled under their windows.
The firewood they ordered was green
and filled the house with smoke.

Raccoons knocked over the garbage cans and strewed the yard
with egg shells and coffee grounds
He bought a pricey snow blower with a two-hundred-foot cord
that broke at once trying to move two feet of ice crusted snow.
As they gazed happily out their picture window at an acre of dead leaves
that had to be raked, a willow tree that had blown down that afternoon,
they sipped Bloody Marys and sighed,
"we adore the country."

The Sweet Life

In the Astro Dermagraphics Parlor,
surrounded by designs of snarling tigers, bull dogs draped in
American flags,
tortured hearts, Amber Sue looked up from
the tattooed fire cracker inscribed "Hot Mama" on her ankle
at a man having the swirls and tongues of fire on his shoulders updated.
Flashing perfect teeth, tossing her auburn curls,
she tucked her phone number into his jeans
before getting into her dented, rust-mottled Corvette
with the bumper sticker "Wine Me–Dine Me–69 Me."

That Friday,
Duane took her to enjoy a fish fry and some drinks at Maddigans' Tavern.
She had a Harvey Wallbanger and he drank draft beer.
Afterward they went to the Red Carpet Motel
in his pickup truck
emblazoned with air-brushed palm trees
and the vanity plate "CRITTER."
In a room smelling of toilet disinfectant,
she had an opportunity to examine the rest of his tattoos.

All summer, they entered contests.
He was a third runner-up in Karaoke at the Alibi Tavern
but didn't even score in the hot dog eating contest at the baseball field,
and threw up behind his truck after unsuccessfully competing
in a chug-a-lug.

Amber Sue easily won four wet tee-shirt contests
in open air bars on the Lake shore
arching her back proudly to the admiration of men mesmerized
by her dripping iridescent form.
Duane watched nervously.

For her birthday party, attended by thirty of her closest friends,
he brought a huge pile of presents,
a four-foot tall stuffed Panda Bear, perfume, bracelets,
and a pair of musical bikini underpants.
Brimming with excitement, she donned them.
Lifting her denim mini-skirt,
she danced around displaying her gift
accompanied by the strains of "Frisky Fingers"
and "When The Saints Go Marching In."

The romance might have gone on forever,
but Duane was picked up by the state troopers for a broken tail light.
A large package of marijuana was discovered
beneath the passenger seat of the truck.
He was incarcerated at a facility surrounded by lush, verdant hills, and
bucolic livestock, forty miles south of the city.
Amber Sue felt sad about his problem, but although he wrote and wrote,
she never visited him.

Rural Distinction

The people who lived in the village
emitted a particular odor.
Not a flowery bouquet or ambrosial fragrance
and not reminiscent of the woods or the shore,
but something unique, specific, indescribable.
At Glorianne's Castle of Beauty
the aroma snaked over and under the pungency
of permanent wave solution,
flirted with nail polish remover, competed with
the sting of hair spray and shampoo.

The Welcome Wagon ladies imparted it to newcomers
along with gift bags of address books, recipe files,
discount gas cards and plastic rain bonnets.
Real estate agents from the city HATED showing houses in the village.
"Scented candles, baking bread, and incense
really add ambiance to an open house,"
they would wheedle
as they vigorously sprayed pine freshener everywhere.
New buyers acquired the essence before the For Sale sign was down.

The recently transferred post mistress complained to her supervisor —
"They all smell here!"
locked her jewelry and purse in the office safe,
refused to leave the building for lunch.
At Antonelli's Funeral Parlor
it emanated from the loved one

overpowered the roses, lilies, tulips
and hovered in the parking lot.

Milky day-old babies
carried lovingly from the hospital
exuded the perfume in their diapers.
Mrs. Pinarski's son-in-law had her front yard dug up.
"It must be coming from the sewer."
"I don't smell anything," his mother complained.
The violent cleaning agent that the local veterinarian used
removed all noxious fumes in his kennels
but not the scent that permeated the fur of the village pets.
The cook at the fire hall stirred his Double Dynamite chili
(onion, garlic, chili peppers)
as the kitchen retained the same village miasma.

Strangers, meeting a resident for the first time,
not sure why they were suspicious,
would inhale deeply
and then smile knowingly.
"Why, you must be from the village."

Charade

They left at five
that fractured morning.
observed only by the foxes, deer, rats
deep in the woods,
the cabin clean
except for a spatter of cold grease
from a ham she'd boiled.
The dial stopped on the electric meter.

The woman, Laura, blonde,
with skin as thin as paper or birch bark.
carried suitcases, boxes.
William, her husband was dark, unshaven, angry,
their child, Mattie,
clutched a stuffed frog.
The shiny red scars on his face
vivid in the early light.

In the spring, Mattie had skipped about the kaleidoscopic yard
chasing sunlit butterflies,
dredging in the sand pile,
oblivious to the snap of a chain two streets above
where Novokowski's shepherd-mix dog
began to forage his way down the hill,
menacing feral cats,
causing small pets to howl and hide.

The dog had been loose in many vaporous dawns
terrifying the children at the bus stop.
The mail man carried pepper spray,
police were called frequently.

Mattie was delighted when it burst through the bushes.
"Doggie."
He ran toward it.
The dog lunged, ripped the child's cheek open and
forced him onto the grass.
Laura ran out of the cabin screaming,
beat at the dog with a rake.

When William came home from work
his wife was cradling Mattie, immersed in a feverish world
of tetanus shots, stitches, bandages,
ghosts of bared teeth, saliva.
Neighbors had driven them to the emergency room.

Enraged, he went to Novokowski's
where the dog slept chained to a kennel
under a moon slipping like mercury through the clouds.
He had a rope.
Quietly, he crept up, unlatched the chain.
Grabbing the dog around its neck with the rope
he dragged it to an oak tree,
wrestled it against the massive trunk.
Throwing the frayed end over a branch,
he hung the animal.

The dog bucked and choked in the bruised night
until it spun silently.

Novokowski came to their cabin door with his shotgun,
smelling of whiskey.
He beat on the door
and fired a shot into the woods before the police came,
slammed him into the patrol car.

The dog hanging trial was held in the village court house.
Animal rights people, neighbors, child protection advocates,
stretched over the lawn, the road,
religious zealots prayed in the grass.
For two days deputies guarded the door.

Inside, a shaken Laura averted her eyes from the jury.
Novakowski and his friends were raucous, had to be admonished.
The windows were open when the verdict of guilty was handed down.
People cried or embraced each other.
Fist fights broke out.
The ambulance tunneled through the mob,
siren howling.

Then the letters, phone calls, graffiti began.
Rocks were thrown at the cabin.
The family huddled inside,
talked to nobody,
not even the ones who had supported them,
left pies and casseroles on the door step.

When the phone call came from
William's brother in Pennsylvania with a job offer —
they packed their clothes, Mattie's toys,
left the furniture,
the empty garbage cans standing in the corrupted yard,
and vanished.

Passages

Hot!
The farm trembled in the heat.
Cows baked in fields deep with flies.
A glassy sun cast red after-images.
The hired man
tossed down his shovel,
stripped off his clothes and leaped onto a farm horse,
kicked it into a canter
through the woods to the swimming hole
where two small boys splashed in the greenish pool under dense trees.
Warren plunged the horse up to its belly,
scooped handfuls of water over his shoulders.
The boys stumbled up the bank
clutching their shoes —
eyes wide at his testicles.

Back at the farm
he pulled on his rank pants and shirt.
His boss, Leona, was serving the mid-day dinner.
A fragrant pot of stew simmered on the stove next to a
boiling caldron of dog food.
The trestle table was crowded with people eager for
potato salad, home baked bread, pies.
Dogs watched beyond the doorway,
lines of drool falling to the floor.

Later, out near the barn with the other hired man,
they watched the kid,
a snotty kid, hired to do some odd jobs, weeding.
Yesterday he gave a disgusted look at the piles of empty whiskey bottles
near the silo.
Quietly,
they took a roll of barb wire from the barn
grabbed the kid and wound the wire around him
snickering at his shouts
and left him on the grass.

Leona was occupied cleaning up the kitchen.
Warren and Howard piled into the farm clunker-
drove past the cornfield
looking for a bar.
They were turned away at Farrow's.
"We don't serve you Indians!"
Last week they'd broken a stool against the wall,
cracked the pine paneling, vomited on the toilet floor.

No one knew them at the Rustic,
a greasy place with torn wallpaper, an indifferent bartender.
They sat apart from the nodding all-day drinkers,
hammered down shots of Tequila, drowsed in a numb gap-toothed haze
while the afternoon washed over them
like a sheet of honey.

Leona blasted the old farm pick-up into the parking lot,
spraying mud and stones against the building,

her gray hair flying,
a mis-buttoned house dress over jeans, her boots crusted with manure.
"Get out and get back to the farm!" she yelled from the doorway.
"Bartender! Don't ever serve them again! They break anything? No?"

The Indians drove unsteadily, parked near the barn
and staggered to where the kid was still trussed.
Fumbling, they unwound the wire.
The kid stood up, stiff-legged,
slapped his pants where the wire had ripped them,
brushed at a few blood spots on his knuckles
and went out to the highway to hitch a ride home.
The Indians fell asleep in lilac shadows on the embracing hay.

Meat

The dusty afternoon was thick with
the smell of suntan oil, fried popcorn and infidelity
when Lynette Coombs sidled past the signs on
the door of Lyle's Stop and Go Corner Store
"NO BAREFEET, SKATEBOARDS. NO PUBLIC TOILET"
in her dripping, black bikini bathing suit
holding her four-year-old daughter, Alana Marie, by the hand
causing the stock boy to drop a frozen turkey.

The proprietor, a goatish septuagenarian
stared, licking his oily lips,
rehearsing suggestive comments.
He and his brother, Claude, who
never said anything to anyone,
stood behind the meat counter
ready to yank out whatever Lynette wanted,
a purple-tinged roast,
crusty meat balls, anonymous cold cuts, gray egg salad.

She nodded to a construction worker in jeans, work boots,
two-day-old beard and his brother, Leroy, wearing his year-round outfit,
a plushy woman's fur coat, make-up, diamond bracelets,
as they picked up their week-end cases of LaBatts and Genesee
while carefully avoiding a broken jar of plum jam
staining the floor like blood.

Near the front of the store, Lucille Krupski, cashier,
was surreptitiously stuffing five-dollar-bills into the pocket
of her slacks
while flirting with the clerk from the North Benson Pharmacy
where she bought her birth control pills,
making a date for the pig roast at Community Days.
"I'll be in the beer tent," she chirped.

In the bread section, a thin woman wearing a wedding ring
pretended not to recognize the bar tender
in whose truck she had grappled the night before
when he left puffy marks of passion on her neck, her shoulders.
Compulsively, he squeezed French bread, hot dog rolls,
kneaded the bagels.

Lyle suddenly stormed up the aisle
kicking over cans of tomatoes, yelling at the cashier.
"Empty those pockets!"
Lucille ran out into the parking lot and leaped into her Jeep.
"You're fired!" he screamed after her.
Mary Beth Fuller came into the store for aspirin
and was hired as a replacement cashier immediately.
"This is the beginning of a career in retail!" she confided breathlessly
to a large woman holding a sack of onions.

Lynette ignored the spotted apples, wrinkled cantaloupes, limp carrots
as she wandered down the cramped aisles

oblivious to the customers inspecting her
their faces hidden behind boxes of cereal.
"We're buying ice cream!" Alana Marie shrilled,
"and donuts and cookies!"
"Meat, honey" her mother corrected her. "We're buying meat."

Tunnel Vision

Encased in the shiny skin of his Mercedes,
the eye surgeon drives to his state-of-the-art office
where he will stride in his white coat,
minister to elite patients, hear
the click of lenses falling through complicated instruments
in his blue, green, brown world of cataracts, corneas, irises.
A master of expensive surgeries.

In their fashionable suburban kitchen
his wife scratches the top off a bottle
and passes out at ten in the morning,
warm whiskey soaking her hair
on the bleached oak table
oblivious to a kennel full of forgiving Newfoundlands
their huge, black warmness straining for
the tinkle of kibble spilled in the bowls.

At night,
the smiling doctor
cheek- kissing through the tuxedoed evenings
at banquets, receptions, first nights, art openings
presenting speeches on rare visual conditions
after oysters, Chateaubriand, London broil, valet parking.
His manicure reflected in the silver cutlery.

"Yes.

She raises purebreds, adores dogs,
chairs many events, benefits.

Tonight? A fundraiser for the animal shelter.
Oh, she wanted to be here, but —

She invites teen-age boys to sexual picnics on the beach
under night-exploded stars,
her underwear floating in the lake,
the sand wet with gin and tears.

In bed, she moans,
the stench of seaweed thick in the air.
Red-eyed dogs howl until
she emerges from under the sea in her nightgown
staggers out
and hurls dog food at the cages.

In his exquisite suite,
mission furniture, and Frank Lloyd Wright, elegant paintings,
he glances at a note from his assistant.
about the next patient,
"Uncooperative"
and finds the woman in the examining room
shabby, questionable insurance, out-dated harlequin glasses — green.
He wipes her thick mascara off roughly with a tissue.
She draws back, raises her hands, objects.

"Your eyes are fine."
She protests.
It has been ten years.
Her eyes burn terribly.

"No.
Your eyes do not need to be examined."

Just Before the House Blew Up

Chickens —
venturing through the night-opened door
perch on the greasy sofa
pecking for lice.
The old man —
wearing six layers of sweaters sits motionless
in the main room of the farmhouse,
staring at a lamp.

Outside,
shaggy steers glare from the windows of a cement and board barn,
mean-looking horses are crabbed against the road
under a flattened moon.
Double rows of fish heads are nailed to the walls of the house.
The porch is full of TV sets, washing machines, radios and bedsprings
crusted with dirt.
Everything is as black as burnt paper.

In the kitchen
the calendar hangs on the wall like a gutted deer skin.
The days have all bled onto the floor,
blueberry pies sit caved into furry segments near the sink.
The oven —
where he accidentally baked his favorite tom cat
hangs open.
His shotguns are piled on a fifty-pound bag of spilled dog food.

He used to hunt in the valley where the hill roads plunged and collapsed,
tonight the hunting dog sits on the barn roof
chewing on a branch.

In the upstairs bedroom
wallpaper hangs in strips where his long-dead wife
ripped out the pattern in a rage.
The closets were torn out by his sons
looking for money.

Suddenly,
the room begins to glow.
The lamp pulsates, becoming brighter.
A dressmaker's dummy lurches erotically against the window,
broken fruit jars fall to the floor.
Thirty years of cracked egg shells
discarded between the stove and the cupboard
chatter incessantly

then —
the house rises like an engorged balloon
chased into the air by the green hooves of spring.
Molten and flaming,
a cinder fist
with the old man inside and the tomcat puffed up like a toad,
it soars over the gorgeous night-struck valley
and explodes into an orbit
circling the stars.

www.ingramcontent.com/pod-product-compliance
Lightning Source LLC
Chambersburg PA
CBHW060500010526
44118CB00018B/2482